MW00946005

THE SEPTOSPHERE

THE SEPTOSPHERE

J.K. P. Antoine

Xulon Press

Xulon Press
2301 Lucien Way #415
Maitland, FL 32751
407.339.4217
www.xulonpress.com

© 2019 by J.K. P. Antoine

All rights reserved solely by the author. The author guarantees all contents are original and do not infringe upon the legal rights of any other person or work. No part of this book may be reproduced in any form without the permission of the author. The views expressed in this book are not necessarily those of the publisher.

Printed in the United States of America.

ISBN-13: 978-1-5456-7580-9

Table of Contents

Prologue

One day in the state of Wisconsin along the beautiful Lake Michigan coast in a town called Port Washington, Aiden Leingold was in school. His instructor, Mr. McPhee, was teaching his class about the elements of nature. Before the bell rang Mr. McPhee asked his students to do a small report about the elements of nature. The class moaned but Aiden smiled a bit because he loved learning about new things and researching topics. A few minutes later, he chose his lunch from the cafeteria and nervously commented to a group of friends that he had to write another report. "Blasted! I have a report about the elements of nature in my science class with Mr. McPhee, which I wouldn't mind except for the fact that it's due right after Christmas break."

Aiden had brown hair and eyes, a hooked nose, fair skin, a muscular body, and was about five and a half feet tall. Due to his father's drinking, Aiden and his father had become somewhat estranged from each other. Aiden was determined not to follow in his father's footsteps in this area. Aiden recalled that when he was a boy, he and his dad went on outings together. They hiked in the woods and did all kinds of Boy Scout activities, such as pitching a tent, making a campfire, numerous arts and crafts, and camping out. He was closer to his mother than his father, and he relied on God to make him a happier person. He was also a Christian and he asked Yeshua (Jesus or Salvation in Hebrew) to bring him joy, peace, hope for a better future, and relief from his sorrows of his childhood.

Intellectually Aiden was an average student who enjoyed learning. He loved to travel to other worlds and cultures via books, and his family often found him alone with his homework or a good book. They also recognized that he had many elements, both emotionally and physically, of his mother, including facial characteristics. Aiden had also been seen running and lifting weights in his spare time to increase his physical strength and also to release his anger.

Later on Aiden said to his friends who wore glasses, a variety of hair colors, and different skin tones, "Mr. McPhee advised us to read and understand the study guide while using Bing to thoroughly analyze the elements." A few hours later the bell rang, the class left with all their belongings, and headed home. While Aiden was home he completed his algebra homework, went on his computer to check his grades, and saw that he had As and Bs, so he smiled. While he was on his computer the family's dog, Shadow (who was a black lab), licked him. As Shadow continued to lick him, he signaled her to stop licking him, then she went away. As time went by he finished his homework and went downstairs for dinner. In the kitchen his mother was cooking and she called him over to assist her with cooking the grass-fed beef. His father was in his recliner, having a beer, watching sports and said, "Hi son, how was school today?" Aiden replied, "It was good, I learned new things and I have a report to do tonight." Aiden thought to himself *I wish my dad had more conversations with me instead of just asking me about school.* Aiden assisted his mother setting the table. A few minutes later they enjoyed tacos for dinner. While the family was having dinner Aiden's mother asked him, "In what subject is your report?" He replied, "Mr. McPhee asked us to do a report on the elements of nature."

An hour or so later he went back to his room and started on his report. When he was about to shut the door his mother quickly shouted to him, "Good luck with your report! Good night." He replied, "Thanks, I love you," and his mother replied, "Love you too."

REALM OF WATER

REALM OF AIR

WHITE MOUNTAINS

DWARVES' HOMES

ELF VILLAGE

GOBLIN CAVE

FOREVERGLADE FOREST

SWAMP

REALMS OF THE SEPTOSPHERE

Chapter I:

Foreverglade Forest

When he sat at his computer, Aiden noticed a strange icon on his tool bar. It said, "Click here for immediate transport." He clicked on it and heard an electrical buzzing sound coming from the tower. The noise grew louder and louder, causing Aiden to close his eyes and cover his ears. Aiden was electronically transported into a multi-colored portal. He was whisked into it and revolved until he lost consciousness. As he slowly recovered from all the spinning and slight nausea, he discovered three other teenagers lying on the floor of the chamber. There were two young women and one young man. When they awoke, they introduced themselves as Elena Savino, and siblings, Dan and Catherine Eisenheim. After they introduced themselves, they tried to figure out where they were. They were in a conundrum and couldn't figure it out.

Suddenly, they heard a voice. It sounded kind, humble, compassionate, but difficult to determine the gender. They asked the voice, "Who are you?" and It answered, "I'm known by many names." Aiden demanded, "Reveal yourself," and It answered, "I come in many forms: a tree, a donkey, or anything I would like to be." Next Catherine asked, "Where in the universe are we?" It answered again, "You are in a secret chamber known as 'The Chamber of Knowledge.' If you say an ancient saying, one of these bookcases will open." Both Daniel and Catherine exclaimed at once, "Can you take us there?" The voice answered jokingly, "I'll do my best". The voice said very loudly, "In the Name of the Eternal Spirit, open a portal leading to a realm of wonder." By saying those words, the runes throughout the chamber started to glow white and a bookshelf in front of them opened. The four teens slowly walked up to it and the voice said to them, "This world in which you're about to enter will look completely different than your world, but it will have elements of Earth." The teens stepped toward the glowing portal. They were swept into it. They materialized into a vast forest covered with coniferous and deciduous growth from saplings to towering trees which touched the sky.

Chapter II:

A Dark Creature Appears

When the teens realized they were rematerialized in a forest, they realized the individual differences they possessed. The teenager, Elena Savino, had an olive complexion, brown eyes, and brown hair with blonde highlights. On the outside she looked beautiful, as her friends said, but she was even more beautiful on the inside. Some of her friends couldn't see it, but after spending time with her, most could tell that she had a heart of gold, putting others first, showing kindness and generosity to others. This was based on her strong faith in her Savior.

The next two teens were Daniel and Catherine Eisenheim, known for their intelligence. This brother and sister used their clever minds in very different ways. Catherine was very analytical, carefully thinking through the consequences of her choices and always placing safety as the cornerstone of her existence. However, Dan had an impetuous nature and was sometimes called a "loose cannon" by his friends.

Their physical features were as follows: dark brown eyes, brown skin, and jet black curly hair. They were of Jewish descent. Catherine doubted that a deity existed and she liked to tell others her opinions. Daniel Eisenheim was a tad more spiritual than his sister. As the teens continued their walk through Foreverglade, they explained that they took high-level classes in middle school and were currently taking advanced math classes in high school. Emotional characteristics possessed by Catherine included trying to think through everything logically and trying to avoid getting in trouble. At times people said to her, "You need to rediscover some things by thinking of them in a more spiritual and emotional way." Similarly, Dan thought through things logically but at times, as his sister said, "He is adventurous and wants to explore." Every time Dan wanted to go on an adventure, his sister rolled her eyes and said, "Brothers, you can't live with them or without them!"

As Aiden, Elena, Dan, and Catherine continued to walk through Foreverglade they looked all around and saw tiny glowing creatures flying around the trees, flowers, and plants. Aiden said, "Those can't be faeries, rylls, nooks and wood nymphs!" Then Catherine blurted out, "There are no such things as..." Suddenly a hand covered her mouth and a female voice warned her, "Don't say that or the faeries will die." She looked up and saw a lovely lady dressed entirely in green carrying a staff with an emerald inside."I am Paradisis, the guardian of nature. Some refer to me as Mother Nature," and she immediately disappeared in a flash of green light.

"Well, that was interesting!" said Catherine. Then Dan said to his sister, "So, now you know not to be so stuck-up all the time and use your imagination." Then she said, "Okay, I will try not to be snooty, arrogant or haughty." She smiled and they continued their walk.

Eventually, a black mist approached them. The black mist turned into a ball and red eyes appeared in the center of the black mist. Then a seemingly kind voice said, "Now I know how to tempt the girl with the black hair. I will go back to the Realm of Shadow and talk to Lord Havoc about how to take over her mind and body."

Chapter III:

The Elfin Village

The teens came upon a village, looked up and saw an archway made of rock. The arch had the ancient Elfin language written at the top. Elena did her best to search for Italian words and phrases, but she found none. The four young adults also saw the words veri il'er. All were dumbfounded and couldn't translate the mysterious words.

The four teens crept toward the arch and were shocked by an invisible protection shield. Just then an elf came towards them and said "Tula sinome" and the gate opened with a tiny creak. The curious adventurers stepped in and introduced themselves to the elf. The elf had pointed ears, long brown hair, brown eyes, ageless skin, and was dressed in a loose-fitting, green robe. Contrary to popular belief, he was actually taller than the teens-about seven feet tall. The elf introduced himself as Finrod, son of Erumallien. Then he said as nicely as he could, "Welcome to Foreverglade Village, where elves can live in peace." He continued by saying, "You sure are brave coming to this world because dark beings come here at times and they cause utter chaos. I'm getting ahead of myself. Can you follow me please?" They followed and he took them through a huge village.

As they journeyed through the village, the teens saw houses that were made of different types of wood. The houses were designed to reflect peace, unity, perfection of self, and nature. Over each door there was a sign in Elfin which Finrod translated into "peace to all who enter here." Elena said to Finrod after his explanation, "It is comforting to hear that aggression is not welcome here."

They journeyed on and eventually came upon a simple-looking but huge mansion. Finrod said to Aiden, Elena, Dan, and Catherine, "Welcome to my humble abode, dear guests." Aiden replied "Nice place you got here," Finrod answered, "Thank you, Aiden, I worked diligently for it." Just then they heard a woman's voice calling, "Finrod, Finrod," and he said in Elfin, "Coming." A few moments later a beautiful woman with blonde hair, ageless skin, pointed ears and dressed in a long, flowing, white robe appeared. Finrod said to his guests, "This is melamin (my love), Ireth Tering, and we have been married for over one hundred years." Then Ireth said to her melamin in a very excited voice "Finrod, I have some amazing news to tell you... We're pregnant!" As soon as he heard this, his eyes started to tear up and he said very proudly "I'm gonna be a father? I can't wait to teach my child our ancient traditions and the Elfin way." Elena asked Ireth, "When will this child be born?" Ireth replied "The child will be born in just over a year. It will take one-hundred years to develop into an adult because of its Elfin genes. I found out that this child of mine and Finrod's was conceived two days ago." Finrod asked "How did you figure out that you were pregnant?" Ireth replied, "Well I went to the healer earlier today and she told me that I was pregnant. When I heard that I was overjoyed that I was finally pregnant."

A few moments later Finrod said to their guests, "Khila amin" (Follow me). The teens followed and he led them to a secret door under the main room. He surreptitiously glanced from side to side, then placed his index finger along the right side of the door and pressed the Elfin sign for peace. Just then a door opened in the middle of all the Elfin symbols. The teens and Finrod stepped into a room and the teens were amazed to see a room full of shields, swords, chest armor (for both men and women), helmets, leg braces, and clothing.

Elena, Aiden, Dan, and Catherine started to go through everything then Finrod said very loudly, "Halt, we must first get your measurements for your armor and clothes. I must first call in a lady who is an expert on fitting clothes and armor." Finrod called out, "Sofie," then a fair-faced woman with jet black hair, muscular arms, and long legs came into the room. She said to them, "I am Sofie, the armory keeper, what are your names?" They replied, "Aiden Leingold, Elena Savino, Catherine and Dan Eisenheim." Then Sofie said to them, "Lets get you in some new clothes that help you blend in with the other townsfolk. The ladies room is to the right and the men's room is on the left." The four teens nodded and Ms. Sofie measured their arm lengths, chest sizes, leg lengths, and head circumferences. Ms. Sofie took some time looking for new clothes for them. Eventually she arrived and gave them simple robes with different colored belts. The colors of the robes were red, blue, green, and purple. The teens went into their dressing rooms and changed into their simple robes. When they came out, they had folded their old clothes neatly in a pile.

Finrod came back into the room and complimented them on their new clothes. Catherine asked nicely, "Why don't we have shoes?" Finrod answered as kindly as he could, "So you don't get the floors filthy and so you can feel the soft grass below your feet." Then Finrod said to the teens, "Since it is nearly evening, we should have dinner back at my place." The teens nodded and followed Finrod to the secret door leading back to the main room in his humble abode.

They noticed that the main room was transformed into a dining room. The table was set for six. The chairs were simple yet elegant, made of some type of wood, and were very comfortable. They also heard harp music coming from behind them in the back right corner. For the appetizer they had salads with tofu, arugula lettuce, carrots, peppers (red, green, and yellow), with raspberry vinaigrette for the dressing. For the entrée they had something that tasted like soy protein with grilled squash, and grilled spinach. Unfamiliar spices and herbs flavored the interesting food. The teens thought everything was delicious. For dessert they had a carob cake that looked and tasted just like chocolate cake.

After the delicious meal Finrod said to the four of them, "Boy, was that good. Do you agree?" The four of them nodded and Finrod rose. Then he said, "Shall we go to bed, ladies and gents?" They all replied "Yes," then Finrod said to Ireth, "Well, mela en colamin (love of my life), shall we go to bed?" She replied, "Yes." Then Finrod said to the four teens, "Your bedrooms are separated into the guys room on the right and girls to the left." As soon as he said that, Aiden, Elena, Dan and Catherine nodded and went into their respective bedrooms.

Chapter IV:

The Goblin Cave

The next morning Elena and Catie greeted each other kindly as they got dressed. Suddenly Elena was shocked to see that her prized necklace that she had received from her nana was gone! She started to cry and Catie tried to comfort her the best way she knew how. She said to her in the sweetest and kindest voice she could, "Elena, do you remember where you saw it last?" She replied, "Si, on top of the table." She glanced at the table-top and below it and found nothing. Then they left their room and headed for Finrod and Ireth's bedroom. They noticed that Finrod and Ireth were at the table. Finrod was reading the paper and Ireth was resting. They noticed the newspaper had both Elfin tongue and human language. As soon as Finrod saw the girls he said "Good morning, my friends, what is the problem?" Elena pondered, then explained, "I noticed that my prized necklace from my nana is gone. Catie and I looked everywhere and then assumed it was stolen. Do you have any idea who might have stolen it?" "It must have been the goblins who always tend to steal something from this village or from other mythical creatures throughout this vast forest. Should we traverse this vast forest and enter their putrid caves? When we get there the goblins will look grotesque and smell horrid."

9

The three of them went into the armory, grabbed their swords, armor, and shields, then left Finrod's house. As they were walking out of the mansion Catie commented, "I see a strange language written on our swords. Can you please translate this language to English?" He replied, "I'll do my best." "The runes you see on your blade are in the ancient language of the elves and my sword is called 'Death Bringer.' Your sword is called 'Slayer.' Elena's sword is called 'Eliminator." They continued on and exited the village. Elena, Finrod, Catherine, and two more elves met at the gate, went to the horse barn, unlocked the gates, mounted their horses, then whistled or made clicking sounds, and were off. Finrod and the other elves commanded "For Rhun (northeast)" and the horses galloped in that direction.

Approximately half an hour later they arrived at the entrance to the goblin caves, which smelled rancid! It was literally an underground cave. As they journeyed downward they heard fighting sounds, growling, and gasses being released (both burping and flatulence). They tried to hold their noses as they saw tunnels going in numerous directions. Finrod, Elena, Catherine, and the Elfin soldiers kept journeying forward and eventually came to a vast room. As soon as the army of goblins saw them, they tried to claw them, and Finrod warned the goblins, "Back, you foul creatures!" When the grotesque, foul-smelling, deformed goblins saw Finrod, they moved back and formed a path leading to their king. When they came upon the throne, they saw the goblin king, who had a grotesque body (with one arm shorter than the other, warts all over his face), a huge goiter on his neck, boils all over his body, hunchbacked, and he smelled horrendous. As soon as the goblin king saw Finrod he said in a booming, growly, angry voice, "You dare to come after us again? You have already slayed so many of us!" Then Finrod replied as kindly as he could, "We have come to retrieve a bracelet this young maiden has lost. Do you know where it could be?" Elena smiled and the grotesque king replied,

"I will never tell you where we have hidden it." Then Finrod became slightly angered but breathed in and instantly calmed down. He slowly drew out Deathbringer and said, "Why can't your kind ever learn to negotiate? Instead, you always want to go to war with the elves." The goblin king replied, "We have no idea what that word means but we won't budge."

Then Finrod closed his eyes and in his mind he said the name *Sorea*. Suddenly they heard a huge roar coming from above. The goblin king said to his army, "Dragon!!!!! Run for your lives and dash to your burrows!" The goblins got up from their "tables" (which were filthy) and ran as fast as they could from the roar. Finrod, Elena, and Catie followed them. As they were running through the tunnels the slower goblins were caught and Finrod said to them forcibly, "Where is the shiny object you just stole?" The elderly goblin replied, in a growly, female voice, "I don't know, but I think it is in the treasure trove at the center of this maze of tunnels." Finrod replied rather jokingly, "Thank you, ma'am." They continued through the maze and eventually came upon a door which had protection spells in the Dark Language of Havoc. Finrod said immediately, "Apire (open)" in Elfish. The doors opened and Elena grabbed her medallion. They headed for the door (which was far off). The medallion looked simple at first, had a diamond in the center, a silver chain, and was made of pure silver. When they exited the caves they saw a huge bluish-green dragon with bat-like wings, sharp teeth, but seemingly kind-looking eyes, which were a mesmerizing blue.

They also saw two griffins, which had heads and wings of eagles, but the bodies of lions. Then Catherine said to Finrod, "Are you sure that these are real griffins and a dragon?" Finrod said, "Yes, of course; touch them." Catie looked at Finrod and the other Elfin soldiers and slowly approached the dragon. The dragon stared directly into Catie's eyes then she felt a weird feeling in her head and Sorea's blue eyes glowed slightly and started to communicate with Catie telepathically, "*Go ahead and ask me a riddle.*" "Okay," Catie said out loud, "What walks on four legs by day, two legs at midday, and three legs at twilight and night?" Sorea thought for a second and replied, "*A human.*" Then Catie said with zeal, "Good." She was going to ask another riddle when Finrod communicated to the griffins, Sorea, and the horses telepathically, "*Take us away.*" Finrod, Catie, and Elena mounted Sorea by the tail. The other soldiers mounted the griffins before they spread their wings and took off into the sky. Then the horses whinnied and galloped off toward the village. They traveled southeast and eventually landed right at the gate. Finrod said to the mythical creatures, "You are released." Then the griffins and Sorea took off for their home somewhere in the beautiful White Mountains. Back at the village gate, Ireth was first in line to meet him. Finrod said, "Melamin Cormamin linduan ele le" ("My love, my heart sings to see thee".) They embraced and kissed passionately. Finrod said to his love, "How is the child doing in your womb?" She laughed and replied, "Fin, it's only a zygote and hopefully it will continue to grow and prosper." Finrod smiled and took Ireth's hand. Then he said to Elena, Catie, and Ireth, "Shall we head back to my place to remove any last rancid traces of goblin?" They all nodded in agreement and headed back to Finrod's abode.

As soon as they returned to Finrod's main room, they noticed that Aiden and Dan were up and ready for the day. The young men called out to the newcomers, "Where have you guys been?" Elena replied, "We were on an adventure in the underground goblin caves." "Tell us, tell us!" Dan exclaimed. Elena told them the entire exciting story about their adventure.

Chapter V:

An Elfin Breakfast

"Great story, Elena!" said Aiden, "Do you have another adventure to tell us?" "No I don't, unfortunately." "Verdui il'er and Quel re" ("Greetings everyone and good morning.") said Ireth, "Shall we have a spot of breakfast?" Finrod, Elena, Catherine, Dan, and Aiden went to the table and saw a simple breakfast on the table for them; they saw freshly baked Elfin bread (or lembas) on the table. All of a sudden Dan and Aiden cut up two to three pieces of bread and started to consume it. "Halt!" said Finrod, "We only eat that much lembas if we ever go on an adventure to the ocean or farther." "Sorry," said Dan. They put the lembas down and the ladies ate a small amount of it.

After they had breakfast they went to their rooms, freshened up, and put on their simple robes. Elena and Catherine came out of their rooms freshly bathed, hair neatly combed, smelling as lovely as a fresh flower garden. Then Dan and Aiden came out, bathed, shaved, hair washed, combed, and refreshed, having removed all traces of sickening goblin odor. Their eyes met as they said to each other, "Good morning." Daniel said to Catherine "Shalom, sister." Then they headed back to the table. As soon as they met Finrod and Ireth, they said to their guests, "Verdui il'er "("Greetings everyone.") Elena, Catie, Aiden, and Dan replied, "Likewise."

Chapter VI:

The Temple and the Journey Beyond

When they finished greeting each other Finrod said, "Shall we head to the temple and thank Yaaraer that our journey was a success?" Elena, Dan, and Aiden nodded, but Catie didn't and she started to walk away. Finrod said to her in a demanding voice, "Where do you think you are going, Miss Catherine?" She replied, "I am going to explore the village." Finrod questioned the rest of the group, "Well, shall we go to the temple?" Ireth said, "Wait, I almost forgot, I have to go to the healer and have this baby of ours checked out." Then Finrod said to his love, "All right, go and see the healer." They kissed and separated, then, Finrod, Elena, Daniel and Aiden continued toward the temple. The temple was located in the center of town. It looked simple, but dignified as well. The temple's wooden doorway had the three Elfin symbols of truth, protection, and love burned into it. Located throughout the symbols were different colors of stained glass. The temple was in a circular shape on the outside and had stained glass windows of leaves, trees, and other elements of a forest. They stepped inside and saw uncomplicated, but elegant rows of wooden chairs right adjacent to each other. Since these were elfin chairs, they were designed to reflect the beauty of nature and Foreverglade. The interior of the chapel contained woodwork which resembled tree bark rising to the ceiling and the ceiling simulated a forest with leaves etched into the ceiling. They took their seats and from a door on the left came a woman dressed in a green robe which flowed gracefully behind her on the floor. She had long, straight, flowing mahogany hair that reached to her thighs, ageless skin, brown eyes, pointed ears and was approximately 6 ½ feet tall. She said, "Welcome, mortals, to the chapel of Foreverglade; my name is Nienna Taratom the amandil (clergic). I am also known as elandili or half-elf. Some of the less educated elves refuse to communicate with me because I'm not fully elf. I try to make friends with man and elf." Then Elena said "Why are a few of the elves so judgmental to those of their kind who aren't full blooded? Didn't Yeshua come to make everyone equal as His children?" asked Elena. "I don't know, they probably haven't read enough about how man and elf can solve things together," said Finrod. "Getting back on target, Nienna, we came here to have a blessing from you to keep us safe from the dark beings out there," Finrod reminded her. Then Nienna closed her eyes and raised her hands above the group and said "Yaaraer (Ancient One), please send down your power of protection over this wise elf and keep these mortals away from the morier (dark ones) and I ask it in the Name of Yeshua of Nazareth, amen." "Nice prayer," said Elena. "Thank you," said Nienna, then Elena said to Finrod, "What do you mean by, the dark ones?" Then, Nienna and Finrod exchanged glances and Nienna said, "Well, we mean wraiths, demons, and shadows. These creatures are from the realm that is ruled by the dark lord, Havoc. They all represent mankind's darkness and evil in the universe." "So what do they look like?" said Elena. "They come in many shapes and sizes. The wraiths are dressed in long, black robes and have pale white skin. Usually they have black hair, long arms, and long black nails. These demonic beings can turn into mist and go up a being's nostrils and take over the mind. Similarly, demons can possess all kinds of beings that are humanlike. Demons are worse than wraiths because they can tell you what to do. They also dress all in black, have pale white skin, regular looking eyes. Adversely, they flash blood red when they are doing evil things, (like torturing people from the inside). Both of these creatures may seem charming and charismatic, so all of you, don't be deceived by their appearance because they can charm you to your doom," warned Finrod. Elena said to Finrod and Nienna, "We'll try not to be deceived, honest." Just then, they heard a woman scream! Then Finrod said, "That voice sounded human and I think it came from near the front gate. Khila amin" ("Follow me.") Aiden, Daniel, Elena, and Nienna followed Finrod. They exited the chapel and headed for the front gate. When they arrived at the front gate they saw Catherine arching her back severely, flinging her arms in all directions, and foaming at the mouth. As soon as Nienna saw Catherine she grabbed her hands and said very loudly, "Yaaraer (Ancient One) Mellonamin (My Lord), come tankha (heal) and koron en'nauer (bless) this young lady." Then she shouted "In the Name of Yeshua of Nazareth come out." As soon as she said those words a strange weapon appeared that looked like a knife of some kind. She pointed it at Catherine and slowly a black mist came out of her nostrils. Then the mist formed itself into a cloud and quickly formed into the shape of a woman. Then Finrod said forcibly to the wraith "How dare you try to possess a harmless woman like her, you foul wraith." The female wraith said charmingly, "How dare I? I was journeying through Foreverglade and I stumbled over this woman who was walking by herself." "Oh really," said Finrod jokingly. Then the wraith said nicely, "I asked her if she would like to know more." The woman replied, 'Yes, knowledge is power.' So I turned myself into mist and I tried to enlighten her with knowledge." Then Nienna said very loudly, "Your kind is trying to corrupt the mortal race, make them evil people, and enslave them!" As soon as she said those words, the wraith became angered and said, "Please stop saying that, oh wise elf." Then Nienna said, "When your kind corrupts humans, Havoc will return and turn this utopian world into chaos, so I say, "In the Name of Yeshua of Nazareth, leave this place." Just then a bright orb appeared. She was absorbed by it and disappeared into the dark of Foreverglade. Then Finrod said to Nienna, smiling "Did you recognize that orb from somewhere in the past?" She nodded and replied, "I do from the Ancient Texts. That bright light shows signs that Prism is returning soon to this world." They both started to smile, then Elena asked, "Who in the universe is Prism?" Then Finrod answered, "Mortals might know him by another name. He will come back, keep the dark lord at bay, and remove the shadow from this world."

Chapter VII:

The Council

When Finrod and Nienna stopped dreaming about Lord Prism's return, Catherine woke up from her possession and shook her head. She got up and said, "Boy, does my head feel funky. What happened to me?" Finrod replied in a very kind and professional voice, "When Elena, Aiden, Dan and I were in the chapel praying, and you were wandering the village when you were transfixed by a wraith and you granted her permission to possess your body, so she did." Catherine replied curiously, "A wraith? What on earth is a wraith?" Finrod explained, "Wraiths are terrible creatures from the realm of darkness. They have pale white skin, usually black hair, and they travel far distances in mist." Then Catie questioned, "So what is their weakness?" Finrod pondered for a minute and answered "From what I know, their main weakness is the inner light in our souls. Remember that our inner light is an impenetrable force against the dark forces in the universe. You can seek out The One who is prophesied in the Sacred Texts to receive the inner light. Have a great evening." "Thank you for that enlightening advice, Fin," answered Catie. As Finrod closed the door, he told them, "Have a safe and refreshing respite."

The next morning, Elena and Catherine woke up and got ready. As they headed for the door and opened it, they saw Finrod standing in the hallway outside the doorway. He said to them, "Quel amron ("Good morning") and shall we go and see the council to find out what they have to say?" Ireth, Daniel, and Aiden joined them and they approached the council together. After exiting Finrod and Irith's abode, they headed for the gate, then turned left and eventually came upon the council chamber. The council chamber was of Elfin design, was open to reveal the vastness of Foreverglade, and had "The Council of Foreverglade" written above the doorway in Elfin. They stepped inside. The council room was round, and made of a type of wood that was unfamiliar to the mortals. On the perimeter of the circle was a huge window. In front of the vast window was an upper level which Catherine, Daniel, Aiden, and Elena figured might be the place where the council members sit and welcome petitioners. Finally, Finrod said very loudly, "Shalom (peace) and Vedui (greetings) council members." As soon as he said those words bright lights shined and four wooden chairs appeared. On the first chair was a faerie who was just the size of a human palm, dressed all in green. On the second chair was a frog which was green in color. It had one blue eye and one green eye. On the third chair there was an aquatic creature that looked human, but had fishlike characteristics such as gills and fins. On the fourth chair there was an androgynous child who had flaming red hair, pale white skin, possessed long fingers and toes, and was dressed completely in red. When the creatures finished materializing and solidified, Finrod and the four mortals bowed respectfully toward the council members who nodded and said, "Shalom, and what can we do for you?" Daniel explained, "We came here to ask for your help." The faerie whose name was Amaryllis answered him in a high child-like voice, "What kind of help would you like?" Finrod said quickly, "the wraith attack!" The four council people looked at each other and conferred for a minute. After discussing the dilemma, the faerie said in a very wise way, "Fin, you know as well as I do, where there is one there is always another. So that means we should have every being in this vast forest and world be on guard for anything that looks suspicious and from the realm of shadow. Have we reached a consensus, council?" Everyone nodded and disappeared from their chairs.

"That was interesting," said Daniel. Then Catherine said, "How could a frog be that big and have each eye a different color?" Then Finrod said, "That frog is one of King Phoebus's MANY children so if any of you approach her, do so in a very respectful and honorable way." The mortals nodded and they went out the huge wooden door. When they exited the door they went back to Finrod's abode.

Chapter VIII:

The Second Sign of Darkness Coming

As soon as they entered Finrod's abode, they noticed Ireth was reading a large book which looked aged and the four mortals could not read it because it was written in Elvish, not English or Italian. Finrod, Elena, Catherine, Daniel, and Aiden approached Ireth, then she looked up and said "Vedui il'er Elen si lumen omentilmo" ("Greetings everyone, A star shall shine on the hour of our meeting"). Then Finrod said to his melamin, "What are you reading about?" She replied, "Fin, I am reading the legends of old and the prophesy of Lord Prism's return. The legends state that Prism will return in the darkest hour and he will aid us in severely weakening or killing Havoc and his army of dark beings." Then Catherine said, "Are you sure all this will happen?" Then Finrod said as he rolled his eyes, "Why must you, as an intellectual, doubt what the prophets said about what would occur?" Catherine replied, "We have been taught by our teachers to question things that were written several centuries ago and try to interpret it for our time." Then Ireth said to Catherine. "So explain to us, 'O Wise One,' tell us about the existence of The Spirit." Catherine pondered for a minute and replied "I don't know, as an agnostic, I doubt that the Eternal Spirit exists at all." Finrod replied, as his eyes jotted from one side to the other, "Well, hopefully we will see The Spirit do things that will help us receive the upper hand, then you will believe." Daniel said to his sister, "Catie, why must you always try to overanalyze anything that comes your way? I used to question if the Eternal Spirit existed as well. So explain to me how a human-like brain came into being. Do you really think that it could have been the mere gamble of natural selection or are we the result of Intelligent Design? I now believe in a Creator and worship Him. Come to Temple. If you want to, you can worship Adonai with us, and read Torah with us. Maybe you will be inspired by what Adonai is saying to His people." Then Catherine said a bit perturbed, "Dan, I will try to become more spiritual, and Finrod, must we go to war?" Finrod replied, "No, we don't Catie, Yeshua taught to us in the Beatitudes 'Blessed are the peacemakers, for they shall be called the children of God." Then Finrod said calmly, "Yeshua did say that, but if we don't react to this rising problem, humans, maybe elves, and many other beings might be led into shadow and this world would be turned on its head." Immediately Finrod put both of his hands on his head and he telecommunicated with Sorea. She said in his mind, "Master, I was attacked by these shadows; I tried to struggle and burn them to a crisp, but they didn't burn (since they were just mist). Then I thought for a sec and what you told me about saying Yeshua's name. As soon as I thought of His name, the shadows started to scatter and a light formed in front of me. Then I noticed inside the ball of light a familiar face and I think I saw a glimpse of Lord Prism's kind face in it."

Next, Finrod said to his melamin, "Namaarie and quell esta" ("Farewell and rest well"). Then he gave Ireth a kiss and said to the mortals, "Shall we head to the armory and change into our armor?" They headed to the armory, said "hi" to Sophie, put on their armor and swords, and headed out of the Elfin village to the White Mountains far to the north.

As soon as they left the village they recognized Nienna coming close to them despite the armor she wore; she had a strange device on her right hip. It was a staff with Elvin runes on it. As soon as Finrod saw Nienna he smiled and signaled her to come to them. Finrod said to the Elfin warriors and Nienna, "Vedui" and they continued to march toward the White Mountains. While they were traveling deeper and deeper into Foreverglade they saw numerous woodland creatures like faeries, wood nymphs, nooks, grizzly bears, black bears, and heard a strange language coming from the numerous kinds of trees. Nienna was speaking in a secret ancient language that very few of the elves knew. While she was speaking that strange language the Eisenheims noticed a bright light coming from her staff. Catherine asked Nienna in a soft voice, "Nienna, what are the trees saying to each other?" She answered, "The trees are spreading rumors to each other and they are talking to each other in a language that is very ancient, in fact, older than Elvish ,and complicated to translate." The Eisenheims thought the strange light and language she was speaking might have something to do with her being a priestess. As they kept journeying forward, each of them saw the gigantic White Mountains getting bigger and bigger as they proceeded onward. As they approached the foot of the mountain, they heard an evil sound coming from higher in the mountain.

Nienna thought for a moment and said in Elfish "open" and right in front of them appeared a door made of solid rock and the elves said "Yaaraer (the Ancient One), give us strength." Then they pushed and pushed, until they were rewarded with entry into a cave-like structure within the White Mountains. They looked in and saw Dwarfish script everywhere. Finrod asked one of the elves, "Can any of you translate Dwarfish?" One of the elves replied, "Somewhat." Then Nienna said, "Do your best." The elf who turned out to be a female elf translated the dwarfish runes, "Elves, be warned: If you enter the caves we might become your friends, or we might not." Nienna rolled her eyes and said, "Dwarves, they are so stubborn and at times greed corrupts them quickly and easily, but they might remember a time when we cooperated to over-come a common enemy. That was centuries ago!" Daniel asked, "So shall we go in and see if they want to be our friends?" Finrod replied kindly, "We shall." The group slowly entered through the small door and the elves, who were rather tall, squeezed through the tiny doorway.

Chapter IX:

The Dwarves Under the Mountain

When they entered the caves they saw stairs and hallways going in all directions. This time however, the stairs and hallways were expertly crafted, and the ceilings were covered in precious metals and jewels. Far in the back, they saw a fiery glow coming from deep inside the mountain, and they listened carefully, then heard the sound of pick axes striking stone and the sound of dwarves' grunting coming from deep below them. They kept going forward and they saw tiny tracks which looked like they belonged to mining carts. As they tried to squeeze themselves into the carts, the group noticed that the carts started to roll forward. The carts rolled faster, faster, and faster, until they eventually came upon a huge room. Far to the left, they noticed tower-like structures which fumed a steam-like smoke coming from them. Directly in front of them they saw a chamber which had expertly crafted stone walls, with dwarf script written in the center and on the walls. They kept moving forward and suddenly they heard creaking metal coming towards them. They looked to the right and saw a laser scanner that could immediately recognize the identity of all entrants. If the scanner identified an intruder, a robot entered. It was powered by steam, had Dwarfish script written all over it, rolled on wheels, and had a steam release stack coming from the top; it had a pressure gauge that was near the back. In Dwarfish the machine warned, "Intruders! Intruders of elvish and human species!" The robot reached out with metallic fingers and caught them; it had a firm grip. The robot also had access to electricity which detained them. A few minutes later the door on the right opened and an elderly dwarf came out. The dwarf had a braided white beard that nearly dragged on the floor. His clothes looked as if he were royalty, but were filthy. He had a lantern-like object on his head, skin that looked middle-aged, and kind-looking eyes. The dwarf's white hair was tied in a braid behind him.

Some of the elfin warriors drew their Elfin blades and some of them said forcibly, "Naugrimani naa essa ellle" ("Dwarf, what is your name?") The elderly dwarf said, "I am known to the elves as Usguener and Gal by the dwarves." Then Catherine curiously asked, "How old are you, Gal?" Then Gal said, "Four hundred, and I am the Rik (or king of the Dawi under the White Mountains)." Then Elena said, "Well, your Majesty." Then the dwarf said kindly, "Please call me Gal if you please." Then Catherine continued, "Ok, Gal, tell us how to get out of this mountain." Then the king under the White Mountain pondered for a minute, then said, "Well, to escape this massive mountain range, you need to journey through our mines, try to avoid falling stones, and try to be congenial to the worker dwarves." Finrod and Nienna said, "We promise." Then the king said to those gathered in the room in dwarfish, "Open, and let these travelers traverse safely to wherever they need to go." Finrod, Nienna, Elena, Aiden, Catherine and Daniel heard a computer-like voice coming from above them. Miraculously, the four young teens heard the voice speak in English and the elves heard it in Elfish tongue. The teens heard the voice say, "Greetings and welcome to the realm of earth. You previously mentioned that you wanted to traverse through this cave and come out the other side." The teens and the elves said simultaneously "Yes." Then from outside of the room they heard something that sounded like a pathway changing in many directions. From above them they heard a whir-ring noise coming from every side of the room. Suddenly, the group heard a strange sound and something that looked like electricity seeking a path around them. They noticed that the strange electricity was encircling them and a few seconds later they realized that they were mysteriously transported into the caves.

When they teleported into the caves they saw dwarves every-where in the huge caves digging for many kinds of precious metals and jewels. As they journeyed through the Dwarfin caves, they saw dwarves with hair and beards braided in every which way, dressed in filthy clothing. They each carried a pick axe held in muscular arms, ranging in age seemingly from late teen to elderly. When they looked over the edge of the stone trail they saw a bright light coming from beneath them. Catherine asked her brother, "What do you think those bright lights are for in the center of this vast cave?" Just then, a seemingly young dwarf came down and said, "Those diamonds you see provide light to this mine and those diamonds were given to us by Lord Prism (the Guardian of Light), who pro-tects us from all the dark beings that live beneath us in the Realm of Fire." Then Catherine asked, "What type of creatures live in the Realm of Fire?" Then the seemingly young dwarf said, "Fire demons (which appear reptilian, have fiery red eyes, enormous wings, thick reddish leathery skin, black horns, muscular arms and legs, lengthy claws, and a mouth full of sharp fangs). The smaller infirits, (wolf-like creatures which have large triangular ears covered in fiery red fur on the outside to match their pelts and black skin on the inside, have long black horns, fur that is fiery red, muscular arms and legs, and sharp claws), lava demons (who like to wallow in magma/lava), gargoyles, and many other dangerous creatures. Then Nienna asked, "Shall we continue tra-versing through this mountain?" The dwarf replied, "Got "(march quickly) and hope you come out alive and unharmed."

The teens, the elves and the dwarf nodded at each other and the group kept advancing through the mountain. They journeyed deeper into the cave, which was growing darker and hotter as well. Neinna folded her hands whispering, "Give me light." The torches were immediately lit by the Ancient One (who answered her prayer). Then Daniel and Aiden simultaneously exclaimed, "Goodness, are we hungry!" Finrod unhinged his pack and Nienna folded her hands and asked the Ancient One, (her Lord and Savior) for assistance once again reciting "Vara Tel'Seladarine (protection)." Miraculously, a shield slowly formed itself around them. Then as the shield finished forming, Finrod reached into his pack, pulled out a bizarre group of herbs and lembas bread. The herbs had different shades of green. The mortals and elves took a few slices of the lembas bread, and tasted the collection of herbs. They tasted delectable. Catherine asked Ireth, "What kind of herbs are in here?" Ireth replied, "These herbs are only grown here and they are maintained by faerie folk. The elves are only allowed to reap these herbs at certain times of the year with permission from the faeries. We can tell mortals the recipe only after getting to know them and trusting in them. Then we can ask permission from the faeries." Next Elena asked, "So did you guys get the recipe and may we use it?" Nienna replied, "Since we don't thoroughly trust you yet, we can't give you the recipe. Shall we retire for the night?" The elves nodded and went straight to bed. They found a resting place within the shield and settled in.

During the night, Aiden confided, "Dan, there are times I think I am in love with your sister and my heart is telling me I want to be with her." Then Dan replied to Aiden, "Well, hopefully you will tell her about Christianity and if she degrades the Lord, make sure to reply lovingly with Scripture." Then Aiden said, "Ok, if we argue about faith, I will try to tell her about the Lord." The next morning they arose and the shield was very nearly dissipated.

Just then they heard a loud screech coming from below them. A gargoyle arose and roared at them. The gargoyle was black from horns to feet. It had humongous wings, the horns were curved, and it had red eyes that were staring right at them. The gargoyle also had muscular arms and legs. On its hands and feet were sharp claws that were elongated and pointy and it was gigantic in size. The group used their individual shields to block the claws and sharp teeth. The gargoyle tried to blow them away with its massive wings, but the small army kept their ground. They tried to stab the gargoyle with their Elvin blades, but the gargoyle was too difficult to stab because of its tough skin. As the fight raged on, Finrod thought for a second about a gargoyle's weakness and it sprang into his head. As the gargoyle brought his gargantuan hand towards Finrod, Finrod folded his hands and a few seconds later a light as bright as the sun protected them from the gargoyle. Next the teens and elves saw the gargoyle fly back beneath the White Mountains as it was turning back into stone. Nienna said to the group as they sat in a circle, "This is the second time that the Ancient One has protected us and removed these foul creatures from us." Then Finrod asked, "Shall we get out of this shadow-infested cave and try to find our way out?" The group nodded and they continued on.

Eventually the group came upon a symbol on the wall of the cave that had a yin/yang in the center with a diamond representing light and obsidian representing shadow. It was surrounded by amethyst, aquamarine, magnetite, ruby, and emerald. Encircling the jewels was an ancient language unfamiliar to each of the elves and mortals. Each of them tried their best to translate the ancient language. Then one of the elves approached the sign and the magnetite-colored gem glowed as a strange gray light started to consume the team. The group covered their eyes and the light traversed them into the magnetite jewel.

Chapter X:

The Castle of the Septosphere

A few moments later they were teleported into an enormous room. The room contained bookshelves with objects similar to tablets. On the walls there were moving pictures that spoke and doors of various shapes.

The six of them approached the bookshelves. They noticed that each book was about a mythical creature or unfamiliar herb. The author and researcher of these tomes was a man named "Ernest Drake." Nienna cautioned the teens to stand back, but before her words could stop him, Daniel reached out to touch one of the tablets and was jolted backwards by an electrical shock. Nienna explained that only an elf can touch the tablets and books. Each is sealed with Elfin magic that prevents anyone but elves from opening them without being zapped. Daniel backed away and Nienna touched the tablets to break the seal and prevent the shockwave.

In the tablets were illustrations and research about mythical sea creatures. They used their fingers to swipe left to right. The creatures they saw on the screens were merpeople, nereids (sea nymphs), sea serpents, strange creatures called kelp dragons, several different kinds of sea mammals, selkies (which are more fish than human) and leviathans (sea monsters). As they read the tomes a voice suddenly spoke to them. The voice sounded friendly and kind, but more demanding. The voice said to them sternly but nicely, "Who are you and how did you enter this castle, brave mortals and elves?" Daniel said hesitantly, "I am not sure how we got here; it must be some sort of illusion or something." Then the voice replied with some sarcasm, "Well, this is new; I guess that the guardians of the Septosphere summoned you here for a reason." Then Aiden said with some obvious confusion, "Didn't Nienna mention that Lord Prism is coming back?" Elena added, "In what shape does Lord Prism appear?" There was a short pause and the voice replied, "He can come in any form He desires and that is why He is a mystery. We never know what He will appear as next because He is a spirit."

Invitingly the voice said to the teens, "Would you like to eventually find your way to the Chamber of Light and find Prism?" The four teens nodded and the voice said, "You have to figure out how to get there yourself." Catherine said enthusiastically, "If it is a challenge, I am ready for it." The rest of the teens nodded. The voice faded, and left behind in the right corner was a dragon statue that came to life. The dragon had yellowish eyes, scaly skin made of stone, and very sharp teeth. The dragon telepathically communicated with them, "Welcome mortals, your first question is… When was the first time you saw a glimpse of Lord Prism?" Quickly, Aiden answered, "When Catie was possessed by the wraith." Then the statue communicated telepathically to them, "Excelente! Now you may move on to the next chamber."

As soon as Aiden answered the question correctly, the wall behind them separated. They walked into another chamber, but this time there were faeries, rylls and wood nymphs. The faeries and the rylls were both five inches tall, wore clothes made of grass and leaves, but the faeries had pale white skin, tiny hands, high-pitched voices, eyes of every color of the rainbow, and many had different hair colors with flower petals all over. Dissimilarly, the rylls had yellowish skin and different hair colors. The fae-folk utilized a combination of things they found in nature such as sticks, flowers, and leaves as clothing and decoration. The nymphs were about five feet tall. As soon as the teens entered the chamber, the faeries, rylls, and wood nymphs gathered around them. The tiny creatures slowly encircled them. Then they asked the teens slyly, "Who is the only god who rose from the dead?" Elena, Catherine, Daniel, and Aiden thought for a moment and went through their minds to come up with an answer. Then the four of them turned toward each other and discussed possible answers. Elena answered for the group, "Yeshua, or otherwise called Jesus." Next the tiny creatures smiled in an eerie manner at the mortals and elves, and the faeries disappeared. When the woodland creatures disappeared, the teens noticed that the room was turning, so each of them held tightly to a stable object. When the room stopped turning, they noticed that they were in another chamber, but this chamber had a beach in it. Near the far end of the room there was an illusion of the realm of water. As they got closer, they saw jagged rocks protruding from the coastline of the Septosphere. From far above them they saw the castle, but it was very faint. As they walked forward, merfolk revealed their striking bodies as they withdrew from the water.

The merfolk had an upper body of a human, bottom half of a fish; both the mermen and mermaids had beautiful faces and bodies. The mermen had muscular chests and handsome faces. One had blonde hair with blue eyes, and the other had brown eyes with black hair. One of the mermaids had black hair with blue eyes and the other had green hair with tiny pearls in it. The teens approached the merfolk cautiously and the merfolk motioned them to come closer. When the teens and elves approached the seashore the mermaids tried to lure Dan and Aiden while the mermen flexed their muscles to entice Elena and Catherine towards them. Elena and Catherine escaped from their trances first, determined to overcome the strength of the testosterone-laden mermen. As the mermaids continued, Elena and Catherine held up their hands towards the mermaids, telling them to back off and reminded the guys to focus on their quest. Next, the two mermen said to the mermaids, "Marina and Aquamarine, we are here to ask these brave mortals and elves a challenging question. If they respond correctly they will move on to the next chamber." Marina replied, "Okay, we shall ask them a question about faith." Then Aquamarine asked the mortals and elves, "What did Yeshua do for the human race?"

Then Catherine said to the group quietly, "Why are these merpeople asking questions about faith, not questions of logic?" Then Dan responded with a question of his own, "Catie, don't you realize that we are trying to find a being that represents light?" Catherine closed her eyes and meditated which calmed herself. Then Elena said to the group excitedly, "He sacrificed His life to save ours!" Marina replied, "Congrats, and you can move to the next chamber." As quickly as they appeared, the merfolk dove back into the seemingly infinite ocean. As soon as the merfolk swam away, the four teens and elves vanished once again in a flash of bright light.

A few seconds later they descended into another chamber but this time they were inside an intensely hot chamber. The chamber contained flame children who had long red hair, pale white skin, yellow eyes, were about four to five feet tall, and wore black flame-proof robes. The fire sprites had pale white skin but their hair was the color of a blazing fire. They were about the size of a human palm (5-10 inches tall). Their wings were colored and shaped like flames from a fire. The sprites wore robes that were fiery red.

As they walked into the chamber, the sprites and flame children floated over to them to question them. "Greetings, elves, sons and daughters of Adam and Eve, "Your question is, what can you do to earn salvation?" Catherine responded quickly, "Do kind things?" Instantaneously the flame children's hair started to catch on fire and their eyes sparked with the fiery color of rage. Aiden searched his imagination for a moment then answered, "Nothing, it was purchased by the blood of Yeshua! All you have to do is accept Yeshua as your Lord and Savior, repent, and accept His gift of Salvation." Instantaneously, the fire in their hair and eyes slowly extinguished.

Chapter XI:

The Chamber of Light

When they reappeared in the next chamber, they noticed that the chamber was ancient and cracks were developing in the stone. In the center of the chamber was a jewel of an unknown classification; it resembled a diamond and was glowing with a brilliant light. The teens slowly approached it and the voice which was very similar to the voice they had heard in the entry room of the Castle of the Septosphere vocalized again. The voice said to them, "Welcome to the Chamber of Light. I am glad you made it here unharmed." Aiden asked the voice, "Who are you? Is Lord Prism in here?" The mysterious voice replied, "I can't really remember who I am, but I think He is in this very room and He is waiting for someone or something to summon Him. You can approach the diamond and see if The Guardian of Light will appear." Next the voice was silenced and the six of them slowly placed their hands nearer to the diamond. When they reached out to touch the radiant diamond, a bright ball of light appeared to their right. The ball of light slowly materialized into a person, Lord Prism, dressed entirely in white with a face that was ageless, endowed with compassionate blue eyes. He carried a staff and on top of the staff was a diamond which caused the peak of the staff to glow. Lord Prism also had long, white luminous hair. When Lord Prism was fully materialized, He said in a very gentle, kind, and loving voice, "You summoned me, sons of Adam, Daughters of Eve, and wise elves. I am known as Lord Prism or The Guardian of Light. Why did you summon me?" Then Elena said as amiably as she could, "Did He really call us another phrase for humans? We summoned you here because Finrod wants to talk to you about the darkness and the possession of Catherine." Prism responded, "Did Finrod really tell you to summon me? Is he here, and does he wish to have a discussion with me?"

Next Finrod and Nienna respectfully bowed with reverence towards Prism, "Your Lordship." When Prism heard this, he turned around and said to his friends, "I haven't seen you in just over a century and how have you been?" Next, Prism said to Finrod, "What has happened here since I left a few centuries ago?" Fin replied, "Your Lordship, some dark things are starting to rise up again in this realm, like wraiths are coming back, and they are trying to bring back the Dark Lord. In Foreverglade we elves are living peacefully. I made some new friends, and I have a small family. That is what is going on these days, Your Lordship."

Afterwards, His Lordship told the group to gather around him. He started to speak quietly in a strange language that the mortals couldn't translate, but the elves recognized some phrases. As Prism was speaking in that strange language, his staff started to glow dazzlingly and suddenly a glistening white light appeared. The light absorbed the entire group and immediately transported them back to Foreverglade. Prism said to Elena, Catherine, Aiden, and Daniel, "Sons and Daughters of Adam and Eve, shall we head back into the elf village?" Prism added, "I know they live a few miles north of here." The teens nodded excitedly and they headed north.

Chapter XII:

Trouble at Finrod's Abode

As they continued through Foreverglade, Prism was leading them with His eyes searching for signs of dark creatures and his staff held tightly in his right hand. As they journeyed through the vast forest Lord Prism said, "Halt, I sense some sort of darkness among us; draw your weapons and watch your surroundings." So they took their Elvin blades from their scabbards, placed their shields on their opposite arms, and kept an eye on their surroundings. From all around them they heard a hissing noise and a snake-like creature came slithering around them. The reptilian creature was entirely a greasy black, with yellow vertical irises, a mouth with two-inch fangs, and a forked reptilian tongue. When Lord Prism recognized the creature, he said very quietly, "Get behind me and don't listen to anything he says." The four teens nodded and the snake-like creature hissed cunningly, "Afternoon humans, and Prism. What are you doing in this forest?" While Prism ignored this deceitful info, he responded sternly and honestly, "I was summoned here by these brave mortals to rescue this world from creatures like you and your master." Then Elena said quietly, "Why were you talking to him in a very stern voice, Lord Prism." Lord Prism responded calmly, "Because Miss Elena, beings like you and I have an 'ability' to see beyond the skin and 'see' their hearts."

Most of my followers who read my Scripture will have this ability. Then she said happily, "So, you are quoting from Scripture where it says, 'For we walk by Faith not by sight", Ohhhh, comes the dawn!" As Catherine and her brother heard that, they made an expression that meant they were confused and jealous that Elena knew quotes from a book they considered loaded with fantasies and nonsense. Then Prism said to the reptilian creature sternly, "If you ever bother any of the creatures of this forest, I will send you back from whence you came and send your master a message that I have returned." Then the reptilian creature returned to the ground and slithered back into the darkness of the forest.

Chapter XIII:

The Commander and Prism's Weapons

Moments later they arrived at the front gate of the village and Lord Prism, who was completely relaxed, returned to his peaceful state. Prism closed his eyes and said to Finrod, "Thank goodness we are among the elves. What has changed since I was last here, and shall we enter?" Fin commented, "Very little has changed here, but my melamin and I are married. One other thing…my melamin and I are pregnant."

As they entered the elf village, Finrod led the teens and His Lordship to his abode. When they arrived, Ireth noticed them, opened the door, and said quietly, "Enter," so they entered the humble abode. As they went into the house they saw someone seated at the table who was dressed in a long black robe with a hood which covered his head. They realized he was tall, as he slowly rose to his full 6 ½ foot height. The hooded figure (who was one of Havoc's wraiths) had pale white hands, pointed fingers and pointed fingernails. The wraith was trying to talk to Ireth but she ignored him because she knew his goal was to create chaos, corrupting all the different species of the Septosphere, especiallly mortals, with his deception. As soon as the wraith saw Prism, he vanished into shadow and left the modest abode. Then Catie said to Ireth, "Vedui mellon!" ("Greetings, friend") Who do you think that man was dressed all in black?" Ireth replied, "I guess that it was one of Havoc's wraiths. How did Lord Prism get here?" Daniel replied, "We summoned him from the Castle of the Septosphere in the Chamber of Light." Ireth said surprisingly, "Oh!" Lord Prism said to the group, "I think you summoned me here at the right time. Now then, my friend, based on what Dan previously mentioned, this world is already showing signs that the dark beings from the Realm of Shadows are trying to resurrect the Dark Lord. If you ask me, we need to teach these mortals how to defend themselves from being tempted and prevent Havoc's resurrection." Next His Lordship glanced over at Finrod and replied, "I am hoping that the commander of the Elfin military will train you in the use of your Elfin blades and shields."

Once again Catherine gave a confused look to Finrod and Lord Prism. Lord Prism saw that she was probably discombobulated so He said to her in a loving and gentle voice, "What are you per- plexed about, and what may I clear up for you?" Catherine replied to Prism, "You previously mentioned about fighting temptation and I am flummoxed by that." Prism answered, "I mean that we fight the dark spirits with our inner selves and if we aren't on Solid Rock, the demons and wraiths will attempt to possess you too. If the Dark Lord possesses your mind, he can tell you (in your mind) to do terrible things to your friends and help him carry out his crimes." Catherine replied, "People like me are unfortunately lacking in faith because we have many questions about God, Jesus, and the Bible. I promise to try to prevent Havoc from manipulating my mind because I do not want to be possessed ever again!" Then Elena said to Catherine, "Why do you two have many questions about Holy Scripture and our Lord, also known as Yeshua to some people." Then Daniel replied, "My sister and I have talked to some people about the Bible and they told us that the Bible is loaded with untruths, manipulated history, and plenty of falsehoods." As soon as Elena heard this she took in a huge breath of air and said calmly, "Do you really believe that Scripture has falsehoods about the past even if it is written by someone who has unlimited intelligence and do you think that The Divine Being manipulates history? I disagree with you." Lord Prism continued, "Shall we continue to the training hall?" The heroes nodded and they walked towards the training hall.

As they were heading out of Finrod's abode, Ireth said, "I wish I could fight beside you as I have done in the past, but I know I must protect the health of our unborn child." Finrod added to his melamin, "Nin mel I na-I best decision an min growing na." ("That is the best decision for our growing family.") Then Ireth replied with a smile. Her mela en'coiamin said, "I agree with you. This journey we are about to undertake might be too rough for you and our unborn child. I am very sorry." After he said that, Ireth got a little tear in her eye, then Prism thought for a moment and he said very cautiously as he removed a small object from his robe, "Ms. Ireth, in my hand is a device that can protect you if you are ever being tempted by a dark creature. Keep it safe until then, but if you need to use it, just say My name and a bright light will arise from it." Ireth replied, "I sure will, My Lord, and safe travels."

The rest of the group traversed to the armory, got their weapons and armor, and headed out the door. As they exited the house, Lord Prism said quietly, "Vara tel Seldarine," (protect) and in front of the door there appeared an invisible shield around the house. If one looked closely, etched in the center of the shield was a symbol of a cross. They went across town to the training facility to see if Elena, Catherine, Daniel, and Aiden wanted to learn how to fight with their spirits and swords. When they arrived at the door of the training facility, an Elfin woman dressed in Elfin armor, with brown hair, fair skin, and green eyes awaited them. She said to the group, "Quel andune and Aaye" ("Good afternoon and Hail"), Lord Prism."

Then Lord Prism replied, "Faelwen, nae saian luume." ("It has been too long.") These four resolute mortals wish to learn more about fighting with swords, shields, their spirits, and their bodies." The commander nodded and she led them into the training hall.

As they entered the training hall, they observed dummies in each corner and the dummies looked like the top half of an elf, mortal, goblin, troll, dwarf, and wraith. The facility had an Elfin design with trees holding up the walls of the training hall, branches on the ceiling with leaves, a pure wood floor, and on the back of the training hall was the Elfin sign for harmony and balance. There were also natural branches and vines growing in between the walls.

Next, Faelwen approached the center of the training hall with her shield in her right hand and her sword in her left. She summoned one of the ladies to come to the center of the training hall. Catherine was the first to approach her. When Catherine arrived in front of Faelwen, Faelwen said, "First of all, tell me your name." Catherine replied, "Catherine Julia Eisenheim, but you may call me Catie." The Commander replied, "Ok, Catie, let us begin." Faelwen stood straight up and told Catie to bow to her and Faelwen did the same. Next Catherine removed her sword from the scabbard and the Commander explained how Catie should begin in defensive stance. Faelwen explained that Catie should remember four important points:1) Start with both feet facing forward and about a yardstick length apart, 2)Bend your legs until you no longer see your feet, attaining a low position giving an adversary less room to attack, 3) Make sure to have your shield as close to your body as possible held in your non-dominant hand, 4) Have your sword at the ready held in your dominant hand. Next Faelwen told Catie that she should block any kind of attack that comes her way. With graceful movements, Faelwen attacked her from above, off to the side, and below, but, Catie blocked every one with her shield, sword, or armor. Shocked, Faelwen told Catie, "Lle naa belegohtar." ("You are a mighty warrior.") Catie, looking confused, asked, "Was that a compliment?" Next Faelwen said, "Did the rest of you get that? I was complimenting Catie on her excellent reaction time to my strikes. I told her she is a mighty warrior. I expect each of my students to stay strong physically, mentally and spiritually." Elena and Dan nodded but Aiden misunderstood, so Faelwen patiently taught him how to use his Elfin weapons in a battle. As Faelwen was reviewing with him, he was thinking, "*I can't believe that I am being taught how to fight by an elf and I think she is lovely as well.*" Faelwen said, "That was the easy part. Now, Lord Prism, will you teach them about how to fight with their inner selves? Your Lordship, will you please step into the center of the hall?" A few moments later Lord Prism stood in the center of the training hall dressed in his armor. The armor was Elfin in design, glowed, and imprinted upon it was a script in Elfin. His head was protected by a helmet, and his long white hair flowed from beneath the helmet. His Lordship also carried a weapon that looked similar to an elfin blade, but if one looked closely, you could detect a shard of the Jewel of Light within the sword.

Chapter XIV:

The Attack

"Now it is time for me to teach you how to fight with your inner selves," Lord Prism instructed as He bowed to His friends. Then Prism said quietly, "Give me light" and his blade started to glow with a pearly white light. Next his Lordship said to the group, "Now I will give this special blade to each of you and we will see which of you has more powerful spirit energy." His Lordship scanned each of the teens to see which of them had more power inside them. His first choice was Elena and when she grabbed the blade it glowed with a dazzling beam. Prism said to her, "My dear, it seems that inside of you there is a powerful light. May I please have Aiden take hold of this special blade?" Then Aiden took hold of the blade and the blade once again glowed brightly, but it started to fade because Aiden figured this blade could see that he had sorrow and darkness in his heart. His Lordship questioned Aiden, "Why do you have such shadow in your heart?" Aiden answered, "Because of my father's drinking, my physical injuries, and the mental abuse I endured from bullies at my school." As soon as Prism heard this, He suspected that Havoc would try to possess Aiden's mind, convince him to join the dark army, and surrender his soul. Prism was irate about the dark memories that haunted this boy's mind; immediately He was sparked by inspiration of what he must do to

49

save Aiden. Prism gave the lightblade to Catherine and when she touched it, the sword went black and she answered, "Like I told you before, I have many questions about the Bible, God, and the New Age belief that all the religions have something of inspiration to say." Following Catie's conundrum, He thought to Himself that the Dark Lord might use her to join the dark army as well.

Seconds later Prism gave his special blade to Daniel and the blade glowed intensely because of his strong faith. As the minutes went by, Prism started to have a conversation with Catie and Aiden. As they were talking, red eyes stared down at them from the ceiling and the demon knew that Havoc was aching to corrupt them and use their shadows to help him come back to life. Next, the demon smiled creepily and disappeared.

As they continued their conversation they heard a noise coming from the door and Lord Prism said to the group in a very protective voice, "Get behind me and have your weapons at the ready." Slowly from the door came black smoke. When it started to condense into a dark cloud surrounding the group, Aiden shouted, "Reveal your identity!" The smoke started to materialize into the shapes of men and women who were dressed from head to toe in lengthy black robes. In front of all the wraiths was Lord Havoc, who was not fully formed yet, shrouded in shadow and still in his weakest form, which was a ghostly form. His head and face were covered by a thick black hood. As soon as Lord Prism saw the specter-like form of Havoc, he said to his former friend in a friendly voice, "Hello, Jay, and why did you come here?" Lord Havoc replied in a low, but crafty voice, "Please do not call me that! My friends are here because we heard that some of these mortals can help me fully resurrect." When Havoc (Jay) finished talking, Prism reminded Jay, "Don't you remember back in school how we used to study about the numerous creatures that live in this beautiful world? We discussed how we tried to make friends with all the creatures, especially the dragons."

As Jay was listening he started to cover his ghostly ears and tremble slightly. As he started to remember when they were friends, the wraiths knew he wasn't strong enough to show his real form so they covered him up in shadow. The other wraiths attacked the mortals and elves. Prism whispered to the teens, "Mallen pelue' sinome." ("Come around here."). The elves shouted very loudly, "In the Name of The One, we cast you out!" As soon as they said those words, a brilliant light came from Prism's sword and as it touched the dark beings, they were turned back into black smoke and escaped through the perimeter of the door.

Chapter XV:

The Meeting with the Guardians

"Well, that was a spectacular show of skill. Can you explain to my brother and I how you did that?" Catherine asked Prism as the black smoke left the training hall. Prism explained, "What you just saw is an example of spiritual energy of the strongest, because Dan and Elena used my light to squelch out Havoc's darkness." The four teens looked at each other, then Catie asked Lord Prism to explain what he meant. His Lordship said to Catherine, "Did you ever hear of spiritual energy?" They nodded and He continued, "Well, when it comes to me, I have the most powerful kind, and as you have observed, my light devastates Jay's darkness. If you don't mind, since Havoc's shadow is growing in strength, we should head back to the castle and discuss our plans on how to counteract Havoc's tricks." When Prism finished talking, he closed his eyes. He started to speak in an ancient language, and folded his hands. Immediately following that, he started converting into the form of a female dragon. The teens were amazed to witness Prism becoming a bluish-green dragon with fiery blue eyes. When Lord Prism finished the transformation, she motioned with her humongous head, for Elena, Katie, Aiden and Dan to come onto her back. She also mentioned to the four teens to be careful of her prickly scales.

Next Finrod asked his friend of more than a century, "May I summon the dragon, Sorea?" His Lordship responded telepathically, "*You sure can.*" So Finrod said telepathically to Sorea, who was a few miles away, "*Sorea, can Ariana ride upon you?*" She answered back "*Yes,*" and a few moments later she arrived with her saddle on and landed right near them. Fin and the minister (Nienna) mounted Sorea. Sorea spread her wings and took off. While they were flying, they saw a variety of faerie folk flying around them. They saw rylls and the Blue Moon Faerie, who was dressed all in powder blue. Her skin was a shimmering blue. She had hair white as ever, pointed ears, ageless skin, was barefoot, and her fingernails were dyed blue. There were also tiny sprites flying around the night sky, and if one looked really closely at the moon, one could see moon fisherpeople who were fishing for stars. As they continued, they looked down and in Foreverglade they saw centaurs gazing at the stars to see what might happen in the next few days. As time went by, the image of the Castle of the Septosphere came closer. When they reached the main entrance Sorea placed her tail on the platform, told Finrod and Nienna to disembark, and the Blue Moon Faerie also landed on the platform. As Sorea flew away, the Blue Moon Faerie said to the group in a soft, sweet voice, "Welcome back to the main castle. Are you here to have a discussion with the guardians about the shadows mounting in the world below?" They all nodded and the Blue Moon Faerie said, "Open." When the mortals and elves landed on the platform, Prism folded his wings and bright light surrounded him as he was absorbed into the diamond.

The teens went through the colossal wooden door. They entered the main chapel of the castle. As they explored it, they looked up at the ceiling and saw seven gems in a circular pattern with an ancient language surrounding them. The seven gems were: an amethyst (gem of air), an aquamarine (gem of water), ruby (gem of fire), an emerald (gem of nature), amber (gem of earth), the gem of light (crystal) , and finally there was magnetite (gem of metal). The gems were all glowing faintly, but the crystal was glowing the brightest. As they continued exploring they looked below them and saw what they had seen on the ceiling, but instead of the seven gems there were seven circles and inside each of them were the colors of the different realms. The teens were transfixed by the seven gems.

The wall suddenly appeared to move! A ghostly figure materialized starting from his feet, and approached the teens. He wore black lace-up boots, plaid pants, white shirt, matching plaid suit-coat and a bowler's hat. He had white sideburns, hair, and mustache, looked professional, and walked with a cane. When he completed the alteration of his form, he walked slowly towards them with his cane. When he came close to them he greeted them in a British accent, "Good day to you ladies, chaps, and elves. My name is Ernest Drake. Have you heard of my research?" The elves nodded but the mortals shook their heads-all except Aiden, who was a voracious reader especially focusing on the supernatural realm, which allowed him to escape some of his dark memories. Mr. Drake also asked, "Can you tell me what year it is?" Catherine answered, "2016." When he heard the year his eyes widened and he said to himself, "It has been over a century since I arrived here and I haven't aged a bit." Following that, he said to the teens, "I can tell you are Americans from your accents and you can obviously tell that I am British. One other thing, may I ask why you are here?" Finrod replied, "We came here to talk to the guardians and can you please summon them?" Mr. Drake nodded, then he stepped slowly into the center of the strange design and tapped his cane in the center three times. Immediately after his tapping the seven gems started to pulsate and from the gems came the guardians. The seven guardians teleported from the gems and they slowly materialized from them. From the amethyst gem came Zepher, who was dressed all in purple, had an aged face, a wooden staff, and inside the staff was the amethyst. From the emerald came Paradisis, whom the teens met in Foreverglade. From the ruby came Mortar, who was dressed in a fiery red robe, had fiery red hair, red eyes, and a staff made of metamorphic rock (which could withstand heat and pressure) with a ruby at the top. From the aquamarine gem came Salandria, who had beautiful skin, blonde hair with a tint of blue in it, was dressed in blue, and had a staff made of driftwood with an aquamarine gem at the top. From the amber gemstone came Gordon who was dressed in an amber-colored robe. He had a broad muscular chest, bulging biceps and triceps, and brown hair. His staff was made of carbon fiber because of its light weight, extreme strength, and resistance to heat. At the top of the carbon fiber staff was an amber gem. From the magnetite came an android named Metalica. She had pale white skin, weird silver eyes, was dressed in a gleaming silver robe, gray hair with bright silver streaks, and elongated arms and legs. From the crystal came Nikola and from behind the wall came a wraith.

When the seven guardians finished their alteration, they smiled, then shook hands with the teens. Next, Mr. Drake bowed slowly. Following that, the guardians touched their staffs together. Immediately after the guardians touched their staffs, a round table appeared. On each chair was the symbol of each realm in the septosphere. On Metalica's chair was a USB cord. As the cord got closer to her brain, it caused her to remove her scalp with her left hand like Velcro, and connect the USB into her brain with her right hand. Her brain was actually a computer with a circuit board, wires going in numerous directions, and the operating system (or motherboard) . Mr. Drake's chair was also of Elfin design, but it had his research etched onto it. On Fin and Nienna's chairs were their names in Elvish; on the mortal teens' chairs were their names in Elvin runes.

A few moments later, Nikola asked the other guardians, "Shall we get to our discussion regarding our mission of counteracting

Havoc's shadow when necessary? Wraith, do not reveal any of this information to the Dark Lord or any of his subjects!" Then the wraith said slyly, "Oh, I won't tell anyone." The elves responded with an angry look at the wraith, Guardian Mortar's eyes turned fiery red, his hair started to burn and the other guardians looked at the wraith with an evil glare. One could tell that the guardians did not trust the wraith because they knew he would give secret information to Havoc and his generals if given the opportunity. Next, Mortar said to the wraith, "If you dare give any of this information to your master, I will make sure all of the beings from my realm use their fiery tempers to torture you anyway they can." As soon as the wraith heard Mortar threaten him with torture, he promised the other guardians that he would keep quiet about the discussion.

Then the guardians and the teens turned towards each other and started to discuss their strategy. They first contemplated how they should notify all the various species in the seven realms to go on defense in case of attack by one of the dark beings. Guardian Zepher was going to tell the faerie folk, just for the sake of security, to bring the mortal children under their spell and put them in suspended animation (a sleep state) to prevent them from coming under the influence of Havoc's shadow. Next Guardian Paradisis asked, "Also, can the trees join us in our fight? May I tell the trees to bring their roots above the ground so they can trip the dark army." Paradisis continued, "Can I also ask the faeries to cause the trolls, ogres, and other disgusting creatures to fall asleep?" She also discussed with the guardians a plan to prevent Havoc from persuading those disgusting creatures to join his side; Guardian Zepher agreed.

Mortar forewarned the teens and elves, "I just want to warn all of you, in case the flame children, the sprites, and all the others cause some of the trees to catch on fire, maybe Salandria can cause water to appear." When Salandria heard this, she looked at Mortar and gave him a look that meant she thought her influence over the aquatic creatures might depend on their mood at the moment. When the merfolk get out of the water, they will have legs only once a month at low tide when there is a full moon. It only lasts for twenty-four hours. If the merpeople don't return to the ocean within a day, they pay an awful price for disobeying the ancient laws. They would turn into seafoam. When the sprites,who look like amphibious creatures, get out they might douse out the fire by morphing into water. She continued on,"The sprites might turn into water only if they are in the right mood to help out. The selkies, who have both gills and lungs, appear to be a combination of humanoid and fish." When Mortar heard this, he became angrier and his hair caught on fire again. Then he calmed himself and the fire extinguished.

Following Mortar's outburst, Guardian Gordon, known for his physical strength, asked the group, "May I ask the dwarves, and all of their relatives to build a fortress to block the entrance to their realm?" The guardians and the teens nodded. Metalica connected a USB cable to her brain and attached the other half to her chair. Then she asked the computer telepathically if it could come up with an algorithm to get the ogres and trolls confused whenever they tried to create turmoil in Foreverglade. The computer replied, "Affirmative," then the android disconnected from the computer.

Chapter XVI:

The Agreement

The guardians faced each other and stood up. Next they placed their staffs together and shook hands. Immediately, a piece of parchment appeared above the guardians and in front of the teens. The piece of parchment looked something like a contract and it read: I swear to try to control myself when the dark creatures tempt me and I swear to defend myself everywhere I go. At the bottom there was a dotted line for them to sign and the four teens signed their names, then the contract disappeared. Since the elves fought the dark creatures before, they read their contract which was in Elvin, quickly signed it and it also vanished. When the guardians saw that the contracts were signed, they turned themselves back into amethyst, aquamarine, ruby, emerald, magnetite, amber and crystal which disappeared out of the main chapel. From the right side of the room, Professor Drake slowly walked towards them and congratulated them, "You four did a superb job and of course the elves did wonderfully. Now it is time for you to join the guardians in the upcoming war with Havoc and his army."

When Drake finished speaking, he tapped his cane on the floor of the main chapel and he materialized back into his ghostly form. Next he flew away, and went through the wall into another section of the castle to prepare for the war. The teens and elves quickly ran to the windows and could see the guardians traverse to each of the seven realms. As they glanced out the windows, they saw the woodland creatures gather around Guardian Paradisis, and they eagerly sought to see the ocean. Deep in the ocean all the aquatic creatures were having a discussion about their war strategy and as they were deliberating about their strategy, Salandria was slowly aging as she needed to get back to her castle and keep her body moist. If she didn't she would quickly start morphing into a ninety-one-hundred year old matriarch. When the mermaids saw this, they carried her to her secret castle. When they entered the castle, they placed her in her chamber and as she was bathing she morphed back to her youthful self. As they continued looking over the Septosphere they couldn't see anything else from the Castle.

A few minutes later they went back to the main door and slowly opened it. They looked out at the night sky and nothing was detected. The teens noticed His Lordship and He said, "I got it, we can meet with the numerous woodland species and form a strategy." A few seconds later His Lordship closed his eyes and he jumped off the platform. As he was falling, he transformed once again, this time into a white dragon. When he finished transforming, the rest of the group jumped on his back and were careful not to land on any of his spikes.

As they were flying, the sun began to set and Prism telepathically advised the teens, "If you feel tired, you can fall asleep on my back and just in case Havoc tries to enter your mind, do your best to ignore him." As time passed, they went to sleep. When Aiden was in a deep sleep, he started to dream. He was having a nightmare about his father's weakness. As that dream became clearer and clearer, a dark presence entered his mind and then he started to concentrate on another memory. The new memory was about when he and his mother were reading. His mother was reading Scripture and he was listening to her read about Yeshua and how He saved the human race. So as the words of Jesus filled his mind, his memories got brighter and brighter .As the minutes passed, the memories of his father started to fade and the dark forces became weaker and weaker. In Catherine's mind she was dreaming about her life. She concentrated on how she could improve herself even more. While she was dreaming, a dark mist entered her brain. As the mist took over her dream, she thought about each religion and what their followers believe. Her memory was jumping from one set of religious beliefs to another, but from out of nowhere there came a quote from the Savior. As soon as she said in her mind, "*In the Name of Yeshua of Nazareth, I cast you out*," the black mist disappeared from her dream.

Back in the Realm of Shadows (which was a hollow, all-encompassing area eternally absent of light), one could easily lose his/her way. There were lost souls floating everywhere, and somewhere, hidden in the thick darkness, Havoc was being brought back to life using dark magic. As he was being restored, he started to be burned by bright light. He started to scream, and one of the wraiths, Morty, said frantically to his master, "My lord, why did you scream out like that?" Havoc replied weakly, "Morty, a boy and a girl used the light of the Savior to rid themselves of my shadow in their minds and as you know, he gasped, light is my greatest weakness. My parasitic needs must be met by finding a way to corrupt these mortals minds, driving them mad while making me strong." Next Morty replied facetiously, "Oh,that is why you were screaming so loudly. Can we continue on your restoration?" The dark lord nodded, and his minions started to chant once again in the dark language. As they were chanting, shadows shrouded the dark lord. The wraiths also offered him a taste of dragon blood. As Havoc swallowed the dragon blood, he became mightier and increased in size. Riding on Prism's back, the teens had landed back in Foreverglade. They were headed to the elf village.

Chapter XVII:

The Meeting with the Elf Queen

Back at the gates of the elf village, Prism said to the group, "Gather around me and we will teleport to the council room." A few seconds later they were in front of the Council Chamber, and they entered through the doors. As they continued to travel to the Council Chamber, the chairs were as they were last time, but this time the chairs were shrouded in shadow. When Nienna went toward the chairs, she whispered, "In Yaaraer's Name, I cast you out." Immediately after calling out Yaaraer's name, light appeared on the chairs briefly and then the shadows reappeared, covering the chairs.

Prism entered, thought to Himself, *"Since the Council has been corrupted by darkness, we should meet with Erulasse and her council to see what we need to do to counter Jay's shadow."* When He finished thinking, He told the group to follow him. As they continued their journey, they went out of the elf village and back into Foreverglade. As they went into a thick part of the forest, the elves said quietly, "Be careful where you step, because as we go further into this enormous forest, we might encounter some shadows, trolls, and many other dangerous creatures." The teens nodded and they drew their weapons.

63

Immediately following that warning, shadows came crawling from somewhere deep within Foreverglade. The shadows were all black, had long appendages, glowing yellow eyes, no hearts, so they had holes in the center of their chests. On the top of their heads were antennae which reached to the floor, their veins were also black, and on their shoulders were tiny batwings. As the shadows came closer to the teens, a giant ball of darkness came towards them. Suddenly Prism declared, "Watch out! Light is their greatest weakness." The teens jumped to the side and Prism exclaimed, "Reflect!" The ball of darkness reflected off his sword and the giant shadow gave out a roar. Next, Darkside came running towards them and when it got to its full height, it was 10-20 feet tall. Darksides' hands were as big as garbage cans and this shadow stared at the teens. Aiden and Elena felt they were being tempted, so they recited Psalm 23. They continued to repeat those inspirational words, which are, "The Lord is my shepherd ; I shall not want. . . Yea, though I walk through the valley of the shadow of death, I will fear no evil." They noticed that darkness was commencing to surround Catherine and she started to falter. Daniel quickly reached out his arm and grabbed Catherine's hand. As he started to pull her back up, Prism lent him some of his light and simultaneously Catherine broke out of the hole. Next Prism told them, "Darksides' weakness is the head, so I would strike his head." The teens nodded and struck Darksides' head while jumping. Eventually, Darkside let out a roar and disappeared into darkness. Next, Havocs' voice made a roar and Her Majesty questioned "What are you doing in this forest, Jay? If I were you, I would hightail it out of here before I send my military after your dark army!" Jay replied mockingly, "Oh really, Your Majesty? I am getting stronger every day and (*one day*) I will return to this wood and you will see me in my strongest form." When he finished talking , the voice retreated.

As he flew away, Elena asked, "Who are you?" The elf queen answered, "I am known as the Elf Queen of Foreverglade, but you can call me Erulasse. Do you want me to show you what I look like?" The mortals nodded and from within the forest came a beautiful elf maiden who was dressed in a simple, but elegant dress. She had long straight brown hair which reached way beyond her waist. Her face was flawless (perfectly aligned) possessed the characteristics of smooth youthful skin, but possessed very wise, green eyes. Her dress had leaves of all kinds etched into it, and she was approximately six feet tall. One could visually see her lean, strong muscles. Those unfamiliar with J.R.R. Tolkein and Chris Paolini works might be surprised to learn that time affects elves differently than mortals.

When Nienna saw the elf queen she said, "Hello, Auntie." Erulasse replied, "Greetings, my dear niece." The mortals were shocked to hear that Nienna was related to Her Majesty. Then the teens bowed gracefully to the elf queen and she nodded with grace towards the teens. Nienna also bowed gracefully towards her auntie, Elena asked Erulasse, "Was it you who spoke to the Dark Lord?" She answered, "Yes, it was! Finrod, do you mind if I take you and these brave mortals to my humble abode?" The group nodded and Erulasse motioned to follow her into the deeper part of the forest. A few moments later, they came upon brush that had Elvin script on it. She motioned the group to stop, then she whispered something in Elvish and the brush slowly separated. They entered and as they proceeded further from the bush, it closed up again. As they continued to walk, they approached Erulasse's castle, which had living vines and trees scaling the walls. It was of elf design, which reflected nature. As they approached the castle, Erulasse opened the wooden door and led them inside.

As they went inside, they saw many varieties of plants climbing up the walls. As they continued their journey, they came upon her throne room, where Erulasses' throne was raised up in the center.

Her Majesty's throne was of Elfin design; it had elf runes engraved into the wood that resembled oak. On both sides of her throne were several other noble chairs and they were also of elfin design similar to her own throne. As Her Majesty sat upon her throne, she carefully adjusted her forest green robe. She asked her mortal guests, "What do you want to talk about?" Nienna explained that they came to the Castle of the Septosphere to have a conversation with the guardians about how to counterattack the Dark Lord's shadow. They said they would help us get the upper hand.

As soon as Her Majesty heard that the Dark Lord would be returning, she spoke Elvish quietly, and from behind her, the trees retracted to reveal a doorway. From the door came other elf nobles, also dressed in long forest green robes, with long blonde, brown, or black hair, and perfectly angled faces. They were six to seven feet tall with long appendages, and walked gracefully towards the group. The Elfin court bowed to their guests, and to Her Majesty. The teens bowed in polite response. Finrod said to Erulasses' court, "Your Majesties, as I aforementioned, we came here to negotiate a plan to counterattack Havoc's dark army. Can we also make an army with the faeriefolk, treefolk, the elves, and maybe the dwarves?" When Her Majesty and her court heard that they might negotiate with the dwarves, their faces showed disgust. Immediately after Erulasses' court created the disagreeable faces, the trees started to move and Paradises came through the trees. She said to the court and the teens, "While I was going through Foreverglade, I could see black slime moving through the trees and shrubs. The emerald on my staff pulsated, which I knew meant that Havoc's shadow was near, so I grabbed my staff with both hands. I could also see the faeries were angered because they hated seeing all the plants being polluted and destroyed. As my feet touched the ground, I shouted, 'All right Jay, I am ready for you; come and attack!' When he heard that, the black slime oiled itself towards me and I stood my ground. Jay started to speak in the accursed dark language and he continued to slink his way towards me. I said in Elvish, 'By the power of the One, help me fight off the Dark Lord. When I finished shouting, my staff shined brighter and the faerie-folk and treepeople assisted me in the fight. As we fought together, I shot green light at the Dark Lord. Amaryllis, the Faerie Queen, told the faerie folk to try to capture him with ancient faerie magic. With Lord Prism's blessing, they captured the black slime , and as he was dragged through the grass , Havoc shouted at me and the faeries angrily. 'You won't get away with this. I will find a way to counterattack this faerie enchantment!' I replied, 'Oh, really, like you can counterattack faerie magic.' Then, he disappeared and I came here."

Erulasses' court was astonished at Paradises' ability to catch Havoc with Lord Prism's support and the assistance of the faeries. Erulasse thought for a second, then asked her court, "Shall we assemble the elf army, the faeries, the animals, the dwarves, the centaurs (which were half human, half horse, with hair so long that it reached the end of their backs), and the mortals who haven't been corrupted by shadow yet?" The court agreed, then dispersed. Erulasse requested that Nienna help her with her armor. Her majesty's armor was designed to look like leaves. Of course she owned an elf sword, a helmet, breast plate, a shield, and boots made by an elf craftsman. The centaurs were equipped with swords and arrows of their own unique design.

Chapter XVIII:

The Army of Light

As they exited Erulasse's secret castle, they journeyed through Foreverglade. As they approached a thicker part of the forest, the elves started to chant in Elfish. As the seconds passed, the shrubbery and the trees moved out of their way. They saw the Elf army approaching with the faeries, sprites, trees, centaurs, and animals of every shape and size; each of them carried either arrows or swords. The male and female Elf army carried shields and armor that resembled leaves. They marched toward the teens gracefully in motions that resembled dancing. The fae-folk also had armor, but it was made of a type of wood that resembled oak. The trees had no traditional weapon or armor because their roots and leaves were their natural weapons; they could be used to trip or restrain the dark creatures of Havoc's army. Some of the trees had grown to two kilometers. There also were fire sprites there as well. Erulasse bowed toward the army, and the army replied, "Aaye (Hail) Queen Eurlasse." The fae-folk and the fire sprites smiled mischievously and Erulasse continued, "Shall we explore this forest? If we ever come across any of Havoc's army, we shall attack." The army replied, "Agreed" and the army marched forward. Nienna replied, "We should also keep an eye out for shadows." As they marched on, the teens noticed that the elves marched in a graceful, choreographed dance.

As they continued to march, the army looked everywhere for Havoc, any of his minions, or shadows. They kept trudging on and on, then a dark portal appeared and demons jumped out of it. The demons had blood-red eyes, sharp brown teeth which hadn't been brushed in forever, reptilian skin, long fingernails, slits for noses, ears with triangular holes on the sides of their heads, and bulging muscles. The demons sensed the army near them; they made loud screams and more dark spirits appeared around them. The elves and centaurs engaged their weapons and went into defense mode. The fire sprites screamed and ignited flames onto the demons. The demons tried to defend themselves but the centaurs used their broadswords to stab the demons while using their hooves to trample the demons. Somehow the demons survived the trampling and being ignited. In the middle of all the fighting, Her Majesty was assaulting the largest of the demons under Havoc's control. She used all of her strength to defend herself. She had wisdom from her 500 years of life experiences. She had trained with her Elfin sword and shield in the secret ancient Elfin arts since she was eighty years old. The trees ensnared the demons with their roots and the consciousness of the trees spoke to the demons. The treepeople used their leaves as weapons to try to cut the demons' reptilian flesh. As the battle raged on, Her Majesty forced the demon on its back and she said to the demon forcibly, "Where can we find your master and where is the entrance to the Realm of Darkness?" The demon replied, "I will never tell you. Havoc doesn't want you to go there because he knows you will ruin his plans." When Erulasse heard this she thought, *"Lord Prism, do you know of any way to discovero the Realm of Darkness?"* She waited for a few seconds and from the center of the battle, pure light materialized out of nowhere and Prism appeared. Next, Prism said to Erulasse, "Your Majesty, in order to go to that accursed realm, I need to get back to the Castle of the Septosphere. Can all of you come close to me?" Immediately Prism closed his eyes and the spirits that were in the trees emerged and went inside of the demons. Seconds later, the demons started to tremble and they began to scream. As they shrieked, Prism placed his staff above everyone and said, "In the Name of The One, I now cast you out." Next, his staff appeared in his hand and he placed his staff near the ground and white lightning zapped the demons. As soon as the lightning touched the demons, they vanished. Aiden questioned, "Where did they go?" Prism replied, "They are in my world now, the Realm of Light, and the spirits in the trees made them think about when they were humans. Their genes are being returned to their original human form. They also caused them to ponder how much pain they had caused in the past." Erulasse said to Prism in a voice weary from battle, "So how will we enter the Realm of Shadow?" Prism replied, "I am sorry to tell you this, Your Majesty, but I am afraid I have to speak in the dark language." When Erulasse heard this she became a bit worried and Prism closed his eyes. As he spoke in the dark language, he kept reminding the others that he was the only one who could use the dark language without losing control of his mind. From his left side, a black portal appeared. Next, Prism said, "Follow me immediately; this portal won't be open for long."

Moments later, the army sped through the portal as fast as they could. When they reached the other side they were in the Realm of Darkness. All around them was total darkness; they could not see a thing. Upon closer observation they noticed the shadows moving along the ground, the walls, and ceiling. Sometimes they glided upside-down. Finrod asked Erulasse, "Your Majesty, is it all right if we draw our weapons?" Her Majesty replied, "Yes." Quick as a flash the army drew their weapons. Then the elves and centaurs drew their arrows out of their quivers as fast as lightning; they also drew their elf blades and broadswords from their scabbards stealthily. The treepeople placed their roots together and minutes later the roots became legs. Next, Erulasse asked the commander "Tira'allara, Mani uma lle merna" ("What do you want us to do?") Commander Faelwen replied, "Just keep an eye on your surroundings and don't listen to a smidgen of the propaganda the dark lord is reciting in our heads." The army nodded and they all checked their surroundings. The army slowly went forward; the faeries tried to use their ancient language to cause light to appear, but it was no use. The trees also tried not to touch any of the black goo that was everywhere. As they continued to march, Havoc's voice started to speak telepathically to the mortals, elves, fea-folk, centaurs and the trees. Havoc said in their heads charmingly, "*Welcome, elf scum, mortals, faeries and trees. I am elated that you are here. Can you please come to my sarcophagus? If you please, can you send me some of your youth to help me regain my strength? Can you please lend me some of your shadow?*" The elves and faeries said forcibly to Havoc, "We will never help you resurrect ! If you want to know some of our secrets of Foreverglade, you will have to fight us for them." Aiden and Catherine were trying to fight against Havoc's manipulations using Aiden's dark memories and Catherine not possessing the Solid Ground of her salvation. Aiden was reciting Psalms to himself and Catherine was doing her best to fight against her shadow. Minutes later, her eyes changed to blood red as she moved slowly in a trance toward Havoc's sarcophagus. As Catherine went towards Havoc's sarcophagus, Havoc, in his parasitic form, opened his mouth. Suddenly Catherine's darkness (which looked oily) went into Havoc's body and he grew in size. As the shadow went into Havoc's body, Prism directed a magnificent light towards Havoc. Prism commanded the elves and the centaurs to fire arrows at Havoc. When the piercing arrows stabbed Havoc, he screamed in pain and spoke in the dark language. All around them shadows, wraiths, and demons slowly crept out of the black goo. As the dark creatures came closer, Amaryllis directed her faeries to gather around her. The faeries attempted to induce flowers to grow and light to shine. As they kept chanting, small bits of light appeared. By recalling what made them angry, the fire sprites made fireballs appear in their hands. They threw the fireballs at Havoc's ghostly body, but they went right through him. The tree-folk also used their branches to reach over to Havoc's ghostly body to strangle him. It was no use because when the trees touched the goo, they screamed in pain and backed off because it was a substance similar to oil which choked the plants. During the battle Erulasse and Amaryllis fought regally but aggressively. The army fought off the dark creatures with aggression and as the battle raged on Prism came close to Havoc's body. When they came into contact, Prism asked his former friend, "Jay, don't you remember when we were children and how much fun we had learning about the ancient tongues spoken here, learning what happens to the plants when we speak to them, and learning about the mythical creatures' anatomy?" When Jay heard this, he was troubled. Next, Jay noticed that Aiden was having trouble so he went into Aiden's body. The elves, faefolk and Prism quickly went over to his body and he started to shake violently. The fae-folk spoke their ancient tongue and Prism placed his staff above Aiden's quivering body. Prism said forcibly, "In the name of Yaaraer, I cast you out." Immediately, Aiden stopped quivering and darkness abandoned his body.

Chapter XIX:

The Way Back Home

When Jay saw that the shadow had emerged out of Aiden's body, he gave a heart-wrenching scream. Prism said to his former friend, "This is payment for all you have done to this realm, you deceiver!" When Prism pointed his staff at Havoc, bright light shot towards Jay. When the light blasted Jay, he exploded. Prism told the Army of Light to hightail it out of there. When they made it out, Prism said to the Army of Light, "Thank you for all you have done. Just in case Havoc comes back, be on guard." The army nodded in unison and went back into the thick forest. Then Prism said to Aiden quietly, "Is there anything you want to tell me about what is bothering you?" Aiden replied, "When I think about my father, darkness comes into my mind. It is a dream of mine to be closer to him." Prism answered as kindly as he could, "Whenever you think of your father, think of Me." Aiden nodded, then Prism said to the other mortals, "Now I need to find a way to get you back to your home world as safely as possible." Prism reflected for a moment then exclaimed, "I got it! Metalico, can you please create a portal leading to the mortal world?" A few seconds later Metalico's voice could be heard saying, "Let me just upload this algorithm ... done." Out of the blue appeared a laser which turned the teens into data and a few minutes later they were back at their computer desks.

A few seconds later the young teens looked at the monitor. The Septosphere icon was gone. As Aiden looked around his room he noticed that nothing had changed. He checked the clock on the monitor; he saw that the time was exactly the same time he noticed as he originally sat down to check his grades. "Now I know what the elements of nature are and I will write them down." So he did. When he finished, he completed his homework, which included Algebra 1, Science, and Social Studies. When he was finished with his homework, he got ready for bed and went to sleep. In his sleep, he dreamed about when he was possessed by Havoc and his fear of being driven to madness when that happened. In his dream, he also recalled Prism and how kind he was to everyone, reminding them to focus on His light. His afterthought before drifting off was his ever-growing feelings toward Elena and he also thought about Biblical quotes relating to kindness.

At Elena's house, which was located in Franklin Park (a suburb of Chicago), her bedroom displayed numerous types of T-shirts from her mission trips , blue jeans, capris, shorts, and a few dresses. In her armoire, she had jewelry which was modest, made with artificial gems. Her walls were painted purple, the ceiling was white, the side walls bore a cross and quotations concerning kindness. If looking closely, one could see that her parents' house was old and some of the floor boards were loose. One could also perceive that members of her church youth group had recently repainted the outside of their house. When she was finished with her homework, she read Bible passages from the book of John and Psalms and fell asleep.

At Catherine and Daniel's house, which is located near New York City, Catherine finished her Algebra II homework, Advanced Biology, and read some quotes by Lao Tzu. When Daniel finished his Algebra 1 and Biology homework, he read from The Gospel of John. While the teens slept, they dreamed of their adventures in the Septosphere. Catherine dreamed particularly about Prism and was fascinated by the kindness He showed to all. Catherine thought about why Prism was so kind; she thought very deeply about Him and she pondered the Scriptures she had read as a child. During her dream-like state, a thought jumped into her head. She reflected back on her childhood and she remembered when her grandmother had told her about 1st Corinthians where it reads, "Love is patient, love is kind…It does not boast, it is not proud. It is not rude, it is not self-seeking…Love never fails." Then she drifted back to sleep.

Epilogue

Back in the Realm of Shadow, tiny droplets of black goo came together as Havoc was reforming himself. He asked his wraiths to lend him some of their shadow, and of course they did. As they did, Havoc multiplied in size. As he reached his ghostly form, he tried his best to stretch his mind and he said to his dark army, *"Thank you for helping me to return, my friends, and someday I wish we could return to the Septosphere to cause additional trouble there."* The wraiths and demons replied, "We can't wait to cause worse trouble in the Septosphere. If you want, we can start out by driving the dwarves mad with greed." Havoc replied telepathically, *"Great idea, my friends, and let me try to reach the minds of the dwarves."* Immediately, he asked his friends to help him reach the dwarves' consciousness. As their minds began to stretch, Prism sensed their presence and said to them mentally, *"What are you guys doing? Are you already trying to corrupt the dwarves?"* The wraiths replied jokingly, *"No."* Then Prism replied, *"Do you want me to send the Army Of Light after you again?"* When the wraiths heard that, they freaked out. The possibility that the army of immortals might attack them turned off their minds. Jay shot back angrily and telepathically, *"You wraiths failed me again, but I will get what I want someday."*

CPSIA information can be obtained
at www.ICGtesting.com
Printed in the USA
LVHW041219150920
666054LV00003B/271